A BETTER KIND OF MADNESS

A BETTER KIND OF MADNESS

Vivid Poetic Images

Deborah Renee

iUniverse, Inc.
Bloomington

A Better Kind of Madness
Vivid Poetic Images

iUniverse books may be ordered through booksellers or by contacting:

iUniverse
1663 Liberty Drive
Bloomington, IN 47403
www.iuniverse.com
1-800-Authors (1-800-288-4677)

ISBN: 978-1-4620-5667-5 (sc)
ISBN: 978-1-4620-5668-2 (hc)
ISBN: 978-1-4620-5666-8 (e)

Library of Congress Control Number: 2011917539

Printed in the United States of America

iUniverse rev. date: 10/20/2011

This book is dedicated to my mother; my brother, Reginald Brown, Sr.; the nieces: Adrien, Brianna, Nikki, Brooke, and Nisa; the nephews: Reggie "Pooka" Brown; Nafis and Damon; my step-mother, Florence Brown; my sister, Stacey Brown; my step-brother, Payton. Also, the Statens: Tall Earl Staten, Lorenzo North, Wanda, Buddy, Aunt Margarite, Shirley and Bud Goins, Della North, Uncle John, Robert and Floria Brown. Also, the Betsy Williams Family Reunion Crew, Basimah and Abdus Tawaab, Melissa and Al, Danny and Dawn Middleton, Aunt Juanita, Mamie and Edward James. With love to you all.

This book is in honor of Parents and Grandparents,
Especially Mom

In memory of "Bookie" (1944 – 2011)

If insanity is what we must accept and live with, then may God help us all to find a better kind of madness.
deborah renee

Contents

Preface

What He Saw

My father was paying his weekly Saturday visit to my house, sitting in his favorite chair, in the usual position: leaning back, with his right ankle resting on top of his left knee. This was a couple of years before Alzheimer's stole his memories, like a merciless thief who leaves nothing behind. He sat with the look of a lion who had just eaten a gazelle and was now totally relaxed and content to lie in the sun—a look he always had on his weekends off from his job at the IRS. In between watching TV and his slow ranting about work, politics, and sports, he blurted, "You should write a book." I looked at him with the same exasperated look I always gave him whenever he brought up the subject.

From the time I was eleven and he took me on our bi-monthly trips to the library for me to borrow new books and return the old ones, he would say, "One day you should write a book, because you have a good imagination." And as a child, I had no idea what he was talking about.

Years later as he sat in my living room, He brought up the subject of writing again I replied, "Well, I have nothing to write about." He said "Write about what you know, or make something up." I looked at him like he was crazy and shook my head from side to side, laughing, because I couldn't picture it; we went back to watching television. Now, over a decade past his death, after the conversation faded, being long forgotten in a faded tapestry of time, I remembered …

Introduction

Frosty air is solitude; and silence expands beneath the weight of falling snowflakes, transforming sounds into smothered echoes. The windows are fogged, barely concealing the icicles hanging from the shingles like frozen rods of crystal. A beautiful and ruthless sight. The sky sparkles as white as the fields. No one is going anywhere anytime soon, including me. Who would want to? At least it's warm here inside, and the tea kettle these days seldom has a chance to cool off.

During these blustery days, I began compiling poems that had been written over the past fifteen years. The original typing paper was dingy and stuffed inside a raggedy manila envelope. It was my secret stash, only taken out by me and read when my mind needed to escape from the world and re-focus on what I really loved to do. Usually this happened when the drudgery at work became almost unbearable. Retrieving my poetry from the dusty envelope and reading it always seemed to take some part of myself into realms of clarity and sweep the static from my mind. And that was a good thing.

About half of the poems in this book come from that secret stash. The others were written recently. I call these poems my "bare, naked poetry", because even though I hope to in the future, at this time, I don't have any formal education in creative writing, no degrees in English or Literature, I am not a Professor in a University, nor do I belong to the "right" literary clubs. I just picked up a pen and a blank paper and started writing. It felt like a big and risky step. I always wanted to publish a book of poetry, but this was the kind of dream that's only real when one is asleep. When I was awake, the dream faded behind working every day, sometimes at two jobs. And then there were the excuses, doubts, disillusionment, and a mixed bag of life stuff that seemed to grow into Mt. Obstacle.

Fortunately, circumstances did in fact weave together like exquisite embroidery on fine linen, and I was able to complete this endeavor. It was a tedious task, but I loved every moment of it. Indeed, writing is an alluring high. I love every word, image, metaphor, rhyme, and simile that gives each poem inside this book its own personality, tone, rhythm, and essence. Just like people, each poem has its strong and weak characteristics and its own unique fingerprint. Poetry is the heartbeat of life and the struggle of the soul that peeks into private chambers inside of us.

This book is divided into five chapters. Each chapter is based upon certain themes and concepts, with its own tone, like different musical notes or colors on canvas. Also, the poems in each chapter are built around certain key words that support each chapter's theme. I use this term, "key words," because like a key, each word would open a new poetic image/idea.

The first chapter is Earth Roads. This chapter's theme revolves around elements in the natural world that we see and sometimes don't see every day. Also, roads of memories are addressed in this chapter. The key words are: earth, trees, flowers, sun, herbs, meadows, mountain, soil, rainbow, fruit, heal, nectar, love, seasons, roads, fragrance, dust, bloom, and colors.

My favorite poem in this chapter is "Walking the Country Road," because this is where my poems are born. The most difficult poem to write in this chapter was "Jigsaw Puzzles," because of its structure, which starts and ends with a short narrative. In between are eight stanzas; each stanza has five lines, and each line has ten syllables.

The second chapter is Fire Shadows. This chapter expresses the theme of the darker, colder side of human nature and relationships. Also contained here are poems with a social and political commentary. You will notice that the tone changes dramatically in this chapter compared to the first. These poems are built on the key words: bitter, hate, haunt, guilt, blood, poison, conscience, fire, justice, hell, heaven, shadow, night, death, pain, delusion, cold, lies, confusion, and dark.

My favorite poem in this chapter is "No Thinking Allowed," because I love the rhythm and stark words of the poem's expression. The most difficult poem to write was "How Fast He Runs," which turned out to be a "prose-ish" narrative. I just couldn't seem to get the words right so that the poem wouldn't sound too gruesome.

The third chapter is Humorology. This chapter's theme is humor and just-for-fun laughs. It includes the *Basketown Anthology* which is about a bizarre, but funny little town, where many interesting people live, written in limericks and mostly rhyming couplets. There are also other light-hearted poems here in this chapter. No particular key words were used here. My favorite poem in this chapter is "A Cat Wears Its At (Out)," because the poem was inspired by all the stray cats that somehow manage to survive on their own. My most difficult poem to write was "It's That Witch," because of its tight rhythm and rhyme style.

The fourth chapter is Water Visions. The theme here deals with all things watery, poetic concepts philosophical, spiritual, and deeper thoughts. The key words used are: rain, water, abyss, pond, brook, stream, lake, liquid, sea, fog, sanctuary, soul, sleep, love, faith, dew, cool, and dream.

My favorite poem in this chapter is "Simply Moon," because its short, sweet tone and images came to me so easily one day while I was vacuuming the rug. The poem most difficult to write was "Visitation of the Gnomes," because it went through about twenty revisions from non-rhyming free-verse to rhyming quatrains.

The fifth and last chapter is Air Lights. This chapter deals with concepts of light and other dimensions, time and space, movement, speed, and sounds. Poems here are built on the key words: wind, butterfly, bee, realms, orbit, wings, galaxy, light, dimension, sounds, dance, mystery, flight, sky, atmosphere, breeze, cosmic, and rays.

My favorite poem in this chapter is "It Vanishes," because of its haunting melancholy beauty. My most difficult poem to write was "Endless Shades of Blue," because of trying to get so much into its short rhyming lines.

In addition, each chapter ends with a poem about the ups and downs of the writing process and the poem's own voice.

Of course, I desire that readers will like my poetry and enjoy reading this book. On second thought, *like* is such a bland word. I would rather that readers allow themselves to *melt* into the poetry, envision the images, and feel the words speaking for themselves.

Well, the frosty winds have now been driven away by relentless heat and the kind of humidity that clings to you like thick body oil. A subtle golden hue of autumn air is already beginning to glow upon the green landscape. Seasons are getting ready to trade places, and whether nature is considered by earth, humans, or the universes, each will continue to write its own poetry. And I invite you, the reader, to take this walk with me along this country road.

Earth Roads

Healing Leaves

Oh trees,
can you spare
a few healing leaves?
I will touch them
with my pen
and let the ink bleed
from wounds.

Bee Lessons

I feel nature's elixir
tickling my tongue,

flowing softly into my
throat.

Eyes closed,
immersed in the sweetness

that caresses my mouth,
fragrance permeates

my nostrils, unceasing,
until my mind clouds

with intoxication.
Joy is held still in the moment.

Warmth pours like the
Sun's oil in an unseen

aura as I become
the bee, thanking

these tiny pearls of liquid,
gold that once slept

in the heart of
the honeysuckle.

Walking the Country Road

I glance back, the view from here is vast.
The long serpentine country road reaches out,
surrounded by stoic trees that are moved only by seasons.

Standing tall as a massive army, the trees' only duty is to shade
lonely roads. Reaching through its winding paths, the road
seems serene but not content, beckoning me to return.

Was there something I forgot?

Knowing mystical roads speak loudly in stillness, I retrace
my paths. The amplified sound of crunching twigs and pebbles,
caused by the weight of my feet, reverberate in the hollow void.

Weary, I kick up dust until it swirls, blurring my vision. But dust
always wanes, and as it does, slowly I recognize the secret language
of old country roads that speak the wisdom of earth and trees.

Now, remembering, I bow to pick up fragmented pieces
of myself, scattered and strewn about. These abandoned shards
I gather from here and there,

long forgotten, now joyfully retrieved, become part of the whole
so I can continue the journey, restored.
And the wise country road nods, smiling.

A Kitchen Kind of Love

we made a potion
brewing with trust,
love, and devotion
in a cast iron pot
of simmering passion
over a slow-burning fire—
stirred it regularly,
seasoned tenderly
with a pinch of healing
herbs and spice,
then added our potion
to the stew of life.
Warm bread we ate
deliberately and slow,
savoring each bite—
giving strength to grow.

Immersion

Morning was sprouting, and with thirst
I drank visions of honey. Clouds curled,

leisurely on the ground, spraying soft mists
throughout the perfumed garden. The birds'

harmony vibrated like a hundred tiny chimes
throbbing upon realms of ether.

The newborn sun, wearing an amber
crown, sent a hint of pale yellow light that sliced

through the foggy mist in iridescent slivers,
causing flowers, leaves, grass, trees to sparkle

like polished porcelain. They all invited this
spectator in, seducing my consciousness with

intense belief that there was no better moment,
or anything mundane more important than

sinking into this ecstatic madness, becoming one
with their serene joy.

Mountain (Diamonte)

mountain,
high, majestic,
imposing, commanding, glowing,
alps, peak, meadow, pasture,
stretching, reaching, growing,
green, fertile
meadow.

Strangers

I am numb today.
Feelings, January-bitten,
are strangers
with blurry faces
that I don't care to know.
The sky sparkles
with unreal cheerfulness.
Clouds wink secret joy.
Even the dandelions,
feathered with thick
eyelashes of yellow velvet,
are smiling;
and I am bursting
with an urge
to step on them,
smashing their perfect
petals into the soil.
Sky, clouds, flowers:
they all look so annoyingly
happy, tugging on
my coldness.
Perhaps I should remove
this burdensome winter
coat and talk to strangers.

Jigsaw Puzzles

The dining room was a tiny square, always stuffy with residue from the coal-burning heater in the cellar. My maternal grandfather spread the box of puzzle pieces on the large rectangular table in the center of the room, a table usually reserved for Grandmom's buttery pound cakes, which she baked and sold to neighbors. When he was giddy with tickles from whiskey, Granddaddy rolled up his pants to the knees and did the Charleston or the Chuck Berry chicken dance. This was a hilarious sight as his long legs and arms flailed wildly in the air. Watching him during these times, it was obvious that he was in some hysterically wild world of his own, and was having a damn good time with it. My cousins and I loved it (Grandmom didn't). We would hold our stomachs in painful laughter and amazement, seeing our usually cool Grandfather act this way. We also loved these moments because we knew the routine: soon Granddaddy would begin to empty his pants pockets of all his loose change; and while dancing around the room, he would throw the coins across the floor for us to dive and tackle each other to fill our pockets with dimes, nickels and pennies.

Besides gambling, drinking, baseball, hunting possum for possum stew, and his skillful ability to suck raw eggs right from out of the shell, it was also Granddaddy's hobby to assemble jigsaw puzzles. Upon finishing, he would paste each puzzle on the dining room wall, neatly, in its own space. Eventually, all four walls, from top to bottom, were covered with his jigsaw puzzles, which always seemed to shock visitors. When they walked into the room, their heads would reel and their eyes would roll around trying to take it all in. As for me, I loved Granddaddy's puzzles and would sit, fascinated, watching him work his magic on the funny shaped puzzle parts. While he rambled on about his mother and his Cherokee grandmother from Georgia and her basket of herbs, her skill at "birthing babies," his days as a sharecropper and time in the Army, I could see his eyes twitching as he held each tiny puzzle bit between his long fingers like a rare diamond, turning it in the dingy yellow light. His mind would immerse itself into some other distant place and I thought I heard murmuring engines that beeped, gearing up with electrical energy that sparked inside his head, as he snapped together piece after piece as though he were joining their hands together.

Thus, I learned that life was a series of jigsaw puzzles; each individual puzzle represented a different phase of life with its mysteries and challenges to solve. Earth moved in predestined cycles, its cosmic story unfolds, fitting together like a puzzle; history stacks itself in different stages, repeating its patterns in new generations. I would help Granddaddy with putting the puzzles together, but would mostly fall asleep by the time he finished. The next morning, at the first scent of coffee brewing, I would eagerly run downstairs to see the latest portrait. And sure enough, there would be the latest puzzle pasted on the wall in its designated spot. For me, this was the best moment … when I could see the total picture. Each puzzle displayed a different part of the world in glorious hues and textures. Perhaps this was also Granddaddy's way of traveling the world. I studied the details through the eyes of a six-year old; and I assigned each puzzle its own story. Time's metered seconds announced themselves from the wind-up clock on the telephone table in the far corner of the room, causing its soft ticking noise to drown out all other sounds. Within the room's bareness, the sweet aroma of coffee, the sharp smell of burning coals from the pot-bellied iron furnace in the cellar began to fade into a distant realm. As I studied the puzzles, each one became a world of animation; and I slowly floated into those worlds. My imagination was born into curious new places of discovery.

I strolled upon black opal cobblestones
in a summer garden, where fuzzy bees
placed honey on my lips and cobalt skies
dropped huge turquoise bubbles; each one was filled
completely with bright beads of the rainbow.

The bottoms of my feet burned as they sank
into golden powder in the middle
of the desert. The sun poured warm liquid
on my back while the Sphinx whispered to me
ancient secrets and mystical journeys.

At dusk, I climbed to the top of a green
checkered lighthouse, stained by time, and watched the
circles of wind cause the ocean to rise
up, salute, and then bow to the tanned seashore
as the scent of seaweed sprayed in the air.

I sat by a fireplace in a hut
and stared through icy windows to observe
the moon weave and sprinkle silver dust on
white velvet and then, with tender fingers, wrap
it upon naked branches and bare fields.

I browsed through an exotic marketplace
busy with colors and merchants. Woven
baskets and earthen jars competed for
coins. Silk garments swung in the breeze, and strong
spices mingled with the scent of jasmine.

In rejoicing, I ran along the bluff
through long, cool grass as the prairie trembled
from rhythms of wild horses carried by
spirit; their thick muscles rolled beneath tight
brilliant coats shining with brown, tan, and red.

I climbed up rings of time on a pewter
tree, held its leaves of brass, bronze, and copper
up to the sky, and gazed at their subtle
veins that shimmered like gold in the sunlight
that caused the green grain to burst through its sheaf.

I slid down rainbows to bounce onto clouds
like trampolines, and glided over storms
on the back of an eagle. Classical
music was the cricket's song; and I ate
moonbeams for popsicles on August nights.

The ticking clock became louder, luring me from somewhere far away. I looked around to see Granddaddy, tall and thin, standing in the doorway. He had just returned from work, and the bare wood floors resonated under his heavy construction boots as he walked into the room. He carried the familiar box under his arm. With a face of contentment, he quickly pushed Grandmom's cakes aside and poured the box's jigsaw bits onto the table as though they were precious silver dollars. As he scrutinized the puzzle pieces, Granddaddy submerged himself in a sea of concentration. I watched, circling on wings of anticipation; and as we hovered over tiny bits of colored cardboard scattered on the square table, our hearts merged.

Aromas (Nonet)

Grandmom baked cakes with pride and sold to
folks who found her cakes delicious;
the fragrance of vanilla
filled the air; when she was
finished with her cakes,
she'd always let
me brush her
long, thick
hair.

It's Like This and That

it's like this:
your spirit tingles for the vision you see, igniting
your soul with fire, the mountain
in the sky is real; and you can climb it.

bombarded with gloomy words from
outside and within, you close ears tight like a
window shut in anger, to insulate from drafts

of doubt that threaten to make a burning heart cold.
a fight against waves of exhilaration and fear, a flight
 without wings, sailing without direction

as the earth removes itself from under your feet.
you stand, misplaced and isolated in thick woods, but
the trudge continues pulled by the gnawing

of thirst, and pushed by an unseen grace.
believing in yourself when no one else does, a refusal
to let go of the vision that's bursting into reality.

a genuine dream and joy of inner being that you
gasp for like air after being under water ... your
longing for it, so fervent, it's almost combustible

like fireworks in the night.
the passion of the spirit.

passion ... it's like that.

Cerebral

worms ate through
the caterpillar's shroud.
melted by the ruthless sun,
he gazed upon fields—
kicked the old paint-peeled
white bucket
full of ruby apples.
his hand squeezed
bruised purple fruit;
the sticky juices glided
through his fingers.
I wondered why he
lifted his crusty hands
to the southern winds,
sniffing dusty gold.
no time to study
his dull ceremony as I ran
to fields of coolness
where colors became gray.
here I lay sprawled naked
upon spongy emerald moss
moist from the sky's breath,
in all my absurdity
a tease to the eye,
cerebral vigor spikes
while I tattoo myself
in wicked obscurity.

Spring (Haiku)

Sun, ripe with yellow
penetrated the soil's chill,
waking tender sprouts.

Bluest (Haiku)

a sacred treasure
bluest beautiful planet
being stripped by greed.

Autumn (Haiku)

They painted themselves
shades of yellow, brown, red-gold,
settling down to sleep.

Anticipation (Tanka)

frozen silhouettes
branches of elegant form
in silence waiting
for the sun's golden satin
ribbons to wrap them in warmth.

Small (Haiku)

the tender green bud,
so fragile; but mercy makes
its life break through rocks.

The Day the Washing Machine Broke

It rose like a magnificent bird, spreading its feathers in various tones of yellow. Hazy steam already

hung in the air like a sheer beige curtain. My paternal grandmother, who we called Big Mommy,

juggled dishes from soapy to rinse water, with a red-checkered dish cloth, which darted

in the sunlight. She didn't just cook food, she built meals like grand monuments; and every meal

was a ribbon-cutting ceremony. She wobble-walked from side to side, ample hips jiggled

like a bowl of jelly in a wind storm, on feet as light and airy as a ballerina's. She used her white

handkerchief, the loyal friend she was never without, to wipe the small waterfall that would erupt

across her forehead throughout the day. Her ears' harmony taught her how to play the piano,

guitar, and organ, a talent she displayed regularly in church. My paternal Grandfather, a porter

and deacon, quiet and reflective, who we called Elder, moved as though he wore bricks instead of shoes on his feet. His Southern drawl and dialect were thicker than

mud in quicksand. They both lived at the top of the charts in efficiency and tidiness. The pastel green

cottage-styled house was dusted, scrubbed, and polished, not a doily, knick-knack, or throw

rug out of place; the lawn and car were tidy, manners were tidy, especially children's; even time

itself was kept tidy, its loose edges smoothed and tucked tightly into schedules. This morning,

like sentries proclaiming approaching danger, they made the announcement:

the washing machine was broken; therefore, we would have to go to the self-service coin-operated

laundry. Linen, colored clothes, towels, white clothes were hurled into their separate bags, stuffed

to the brim. Like fishing days, this was a task to be completed before the bees and grasshoppers

woke up and the Florida sun caused the air to become gorged like a fiery furnace. We loaded

ourselves into the old blue station wagon with wood side panels, an ugly car, built as though the manufacturers couldn't decide whether to build a steel machine or a wooden horse buggy.

Certainly, the car moved along as though it was being pulled by old horses, the tailpipe

almost kissing the dusty ground. So we chugged along, snailing on roads unfamiliar, in

search of a laundromat to transform messy bundles into clean, starched, and folded stacks,

suitable to insert into dresser drawers, on closet shelves and naked clothes hangers. I

knew nothing of being a Jim Crow child, nor did I understand why some neighbors just seemed

to up and disappear, or the meaning of those strange tales that grown-ups whispered

about the widows who wept by the weeping willow trees. At the moment, child

thoughts revolved around thoughts of getting back home to search for frogs and tadpoles,

or chase little helicopter dragonflies, roll in the cool grass, and dirty more clothes. Our car

slowed in front of a neat little box-shaped laundromat. My grandparents, quick and sharply, demanded that the back car windows were to be rolled up. That's when my eyes fell on

them: men in a crowd, as though it was a Saturday night celebration. Indeed, some of them

looked like they had been up all night, with suitcases under their eyes in leather folds,

dingy stained t-shirts that hugged sweaty and sun-peeled skin … skin that magically kept

turning into deeper red shades, right before my amazed seven-year-old eyes. It was my very

first sighting of real white people, except for my first grade teacher, whose gray hair

was always pulled into a bun at the back of her head. But her face was always clean, with

red circles that sat on each cheek, and another across her face where her lips

were supposed to be. But these white folks looked different, painted and plastered

in dirty streaks across their bodies. With eyes that flashed warning signs, they surrounded the car.

Some of them were chewing brown grains, and liquid hung on their mustaches and their teeth and lips, like smeared fudge. Brown slime was propelled from their mouths like

projectiles that landed on our car windows, melting and oozing into streaks, like chocolate

candy on hot asphalt. All together they yelled, their voices raised in an angry pitch,

the sounds buffered by the windows. Enraged as a wild fire sprinting across a dry

field, they waved signs that read, "NO COLOREDS! WHITES ONLY!" In my stunned

eyes, their faces looked like cold stones that sat on top of old bones; perhaps vultures

had picked holes in their brains, from which all light had escaped. Frozen into stillness, I

thought surely they would have eaten us if it weren't for the refuge of an ugly car that at the

moment became the most beautiful place to be. Elder drove steadily; his face never moved

left or right; Big Mommy's eyes also pointed ahead as though the mean men were invisible; and for

a moment I thought I was the only one who could see them. Soon the crowd was in the rear, and another laundromat appeared. The same ghastly scene was repeated with

a different group of white men, waving the same signs: "NO COLOREDS! WHITES ONLY!"

With their skin covered with dirt and red rage, from my child's view, they looked scarier

than the monsters in the Godzilla movies at the Saturday matinee. The next two laundromats

repeated the same repulsive scene, until finally … the road's stripes became longer ribbons

from the car's rear window, the town became smaller, disappearing into the distance,

and the tired muffler's smoke. With happy relief, I felt tension dissipate from inside

the car like steam from boiling water; yet in my child thoughts I couldn't understand

why the folks in a town with so many laundromats wouldn't allow us to wash
our colored clothes.

Rainbow

I feel warm, tranquil
or hot and burning.
Taste me and I will burst
with sour effervescence
in your mouth,
causing your teeth to shutter
and bring tears to your eyes,
yet I am always life-giving.
I signify joy.
I am soft, yet overwhelming.
So brightly I shine,
I could make you blind,
and my scent will magically
lighten your mind. My
sounds make the spirit
quicken with hope.
To buttercups, sunflowers,
and gold I give color, bringing
peaceful hues pure and mellow.
My name is yellow.

Rainbow

I feel cooling, soothing.
Immerse yourself
totally in me and you
will be purified.
I infuse water to sparkle
as a fluid jewel, as I
expand myself in every sea.
Taste me and I will refresh
your mouth, quench thirst
and make your insides shiver.
I can be cold and icy, too.
Sadness is sometimes
called by my name, though
I am always healing
to the eyes. I stand strong
upon the earth, seen from
the outer realms
of the galaxy. I am
the sound that calms
the subconscious mind.
I give glory to
the morning glories,
indigo, amethyst,
and sapphire
get their color from me.
Look up;
I stretch myself out
high above you.
My name is blue.

Rainbow

Unripe, new.
In me dwell yellow and blue.
I wrap my arms
around spring, my season
of celebration.
I wax each blade of grass
and nurture each leaf.
The opulence of earth is
my abode. I am the
atmospheric sustainer.
My taste and aroma
are like spearmint cooling,
tingling to your nose.
I signify the freshness
of new beginnings.
My sounds open the mind
to invigorate.
Feel me; I am the shade
from the burning sun.
Leaves, jade, limes, and
emeralds show off my glory.
I sway in the tree tops.
Tender, fresh, clean.
My name is green.

Rainbow

Hot, fiery,
tempestuous too!
I am never cool
like blue.
Passionate and saucy.
I will always entice
your senses, because I
am bold and daring.
When I darken myself,
I am intoxicating
and enchanting.
If I lighten myself,
I am gentle as a baby.
My sounds stimulate
you to move and dance
because I give all energy
its strength.
My taste is spicy and robust.
I flow through your body,
bringing life.
Roses, garnets, cherries,
and rubies are my best-
known friends.
I signify the heart that
is inflamed with passion.
Crimson, scarlet,
about me
it has all been said!
My name is red.

Rainbow

Bright, sprightly, sharp.
I bounce, dance, and dart.
I can be blinding like
yellow, or fiery like red,
for they are both found
in me. My fingers
twirl in the heat
that burns the flame.
I crawl inside the earth's lava.
My aroma is like citrus.
I taste sour, though sweet.
I resurrect and calm.
My sounds are always uplifting,
and I move in flashes
captivating to your eyes.
In autumn I strut my glory
and paint the landscape.
I shine in copper, and clothe
the marigolds.
My curtains open
with the sunrise,
and I slowly curl behind
the night at sunset.
Proud to brighten and cleanse.
My name is orange.

Rainbow

Royal, regal, dignified.
I can swallow
you in my unknown depths.
In me red and blue
reign supreme.
My scent wafts
as lavender perfume
through open fields.
I taste like the ripe fruit
of the vine
that brims with sweetness
in your mouth.
My sounds resound
with the quiet vibrations of the soul.
Feel me, and I
am cool velvet to your fingertips.
In my darkness,
I adorn the skies
in the hour before dawn,
yet I can lighten myself
and bring freshness to
the azalea and iris, and sparkle
to the amethyst.
Me? I never go unnoticed
before your eyes.
Bold, strong, noble.
My name is purple.

All The Rainbow Children

Heavy, mysterious.
Light and airy.
Some might even
find me scary.
I signify omnipresent
opulence.

Inside me is the rumbling
of thunder to tell you
that the storm is near.
Taste me and you will
become weightless
in time and space.

When I descend,
so does sleep. I hide in
shadows of the deep.
Brilliant stars of the sky
are pulled to me
when they die.

The secret of my mystery
is that even though
you cannot see, all rainbow
children dwell in me.
I am the matter
that is densely dark,
woven through
the universes.

When I flow in liquid gold,
I am ardently desired.
When I fling myself in the
funnel cloud,
I am greatly dreaded.

I signify infinity,
the sum total of the cosmic
energy.

My home is in the strongest
iron or the most delicate pearl
and I shine in the obsidian.
I am seen, yet
incomprehensible.
Of all the colors of the world,
none of them I lack.
My name is black.

Earth

Expansive fields
sway to an unheard
elegy of soft grasses that
have become prickly spindles;
delicate flowers now stab me with
thorns. Sweet waters are bitter, choking
with slime. I wailed for my children who fled
to the west winds, scattered in distress, while many
died trapped under the fetters of harsh duress. I am
a scarred captive in my own home, spiraling off-balance
as useless debris.. My havens are tortured every day, squeezed in
the backwardness of progress until I snap and lash back, destruction
in exchange for ruin. I flail against insults with my four forces until it is
understood that I also am a living entity and I will have a voice because
I
am stronger.

Hospice Sunsets

the shriveled rose,
edges cracked and split,
fell into small bits
of fragrance that floated
into sunset breezes.
green stems faded to thin
brown straws, while death
prepared its path and
reached inside the clock
to seize time's trek.
silence smothered the room.
waiting dragged itself
like a cumbersome chain.
jagged petals wilted
into dried specks of weightless
powder free from matter.
a circular energy pulled
through the exit portal.

Seasons

Summer was a time
We shared.
When the day is hottest, ripe fruit
Sweet to the palate, nectar flowing
From flowers in full bloom
For seasons of love.

Time brought autumn,
When we began to fade away
As trees yellowed to auburn, frayed
Leaves fell on hardened ground.

Winter followed.
A cold wind on brittle bones
Frigid beneath the snow, upon
Layers of the ice of separation,
Lost in an abysmal storm.

Seasons and emotions later,
Spring returned warmth.
Trees and flowers, deadened
From the winter's cold blizzards
Revived and blossomed again.

With memories, emotions evolve

Thawing within our souls.
Hope rising as the sun
On a spring morning, blazing
Hot in full glory on a summer noon.
Just us two ... and seasons.

Betsy Williams

Crumbs in the Wind

You asked what it was like so I'll tell you. Here's the letter from your
Great-great-grandmother that I'm sending through curtains of time and

space: the ink dried on yellow, cracked paper; visions of a better future
drifted as ash sprinkled in the air, fell like frozen flakes you try to hold

but they melt. The noose was kept in our vision as a tight death
claw that grew battered branches from pure trees whose sap was blood.

White sheets that wore dead eyes were watchmen in the night.
We walked against fickle winds, stumbled in thick waters, and stayed

alive anyway, in spite of being forgotten, laborers for wages of burdens,
even as our feet sank deep in plantation soil where dreams were buried.

Oppression was like hot sun we wore on our shoulders. With thorn-
scratched hands, we remained humane, and snatched crumbs of hope to

see if even the smallest bits of justice might taste like the sweetness of
ripe berries, but we were placed in our graves still hungry for those
berries ...

Contentment

they slowly undress
then cover
with an ivory quilt
and sleep in contentment
until their cradle rotates
and warm kisses awaken them.
their peace rests in the faith
that they never strive
to be anything
other than who they are,
or ever think anything lesser
of themselves,
and all are blessed by
their presence
and take refuge
in their strength.
they are true purveyors
of wisdom,
but do people listen
to the trees?

Folded

flowers folded,
hardened beads
napping beneath
trampled soil
unfold, reach
up to bloom,
beauty illuminated
and angels do
walk the earth.

Far Away

I saw a mountain in the sky.
A mystic pillar standing high.
Fire covered its purple gown
On horizons dressed to glorify.

Orange streaks and lavender crown.
Its silver fog comforts the eye.
I ride this mountain, looking down
On earth below, swirling around.

Lay Down Your Soul on Me

It meets my eyes, a vacant stare.
In nakedness, it seems so bare.

What more of life is there to write?
Sunsets, dawn, or the lovers' plight?

Plethora of words prance and tease,
Seduce my heart, but give no ease,

Instead run wild, like weeds untamed
They have no form, no home or name.

Blank paper mourns like barren lands
Then softly speaks through outstretched hands—

"I'm fallow, yes, but I shall speak
Of secret potions that you seek.

Just trust: lay down your soul on me.
The muse will gush forth fruitfully.

Complete me with your seeds of lore,
Open wide the sequestered door.

Let your passion descend like rain
Upon this paper's barren plain.

For when your mind guides what you know,
These bare pages sprout like meadows."

Fire Shadows

Diet

free yourself from sharp claws
while your days have time
gather all the nasty food
expel it from your mind

Tea-zeezed (Senryu)

the tea was poison
but they drank it anyway
and became diseased.

ꝑ Deborah Renee

The Keeper of the Garden

Her hands are razors;
venom dribbles from her mouth.
Strong eyes always searching
for the jugular, while

her heart swings between
love and loathing, bouncing upon
inner walls of misery.
She laughs while slicing through

the vines of ripe, sweet fruit,
ripping up dreams of flowering
buds, plucking colorful petals.
Immersing herself in a fountain

of dominance, she tramples upon
hopeful seedlings, until all life is
smothered and her anger is satiated.
After years of leftover chaos,

the stormy remnants of weeping
buds, torn petals of promise, spineless
seedlings, and hearts of tangled
vines, now captive, lay sprawled

at her feet as willing captives. With weak
eyes she weeps, unaware of what happened
to her garden, as she tells herself
that at least now she won't be bitter alone.

Maggots and the Carcass

They appoint themselves, sitting bold in
The circle of authority, cold, hollow
Fiends veiled behind the caricatures
Of human faces whose crimes leave
Bitter fruit without guilty traces.

Deciding on perverted whims who's worthy
To rise to heights and survive,
Who dies or gets tossed to the side
As grunts, crawling, grabbing for crumbs,
And struggling to stay alive.

They whisper seduction eloquently or shout
Vociferously as the masses' clarity melts
Into cloudiness and willingness to believe
Anything … just don't tell us that we've lost
Our way, but let us play. We'll pledge allegiance

To the lies you place in our empty hands,
Pretending we live in a perfect wonderland.
As myriads of trinkets and trifles progress,
Humaneness suffers and reverses its steps.
As knowledge increases in external spheres,

Poison overtakes the internal fears.
How can we unbind ourselves from illusions
When we dread the other side of delusion?
So, unobstructed, they continue to dance in towers
Of power; filthy maggots that devour

The rotting carcass of humanity.
Preaching, explaining, that insanity is sanity.
Wolves, all of them, insatiable for rule, dripping
With blood, sharpen their tools
And invite howling sheep to the slaughter.

The Old Man on the Porch

Tempers blast hot, cool with apologies,

two separate pieces of weary, faded

fiber woven together in intricate tapestries.

Mouths once full of smiles now hold

clenched teeth. Sweethearts through days

of elation grew into a pit of cold glares,

tired stares. Limbs once intertwined in heat,

now lock together as fierce weapons.

He kept his secret guarded well. Her

expressionless face carved on the bottom

of the hall's wooden stairs engraved itself in

his mind. Neighbors buzzed about it being a

shame, such a tragic slip of her foot.

Daily, on his porch, he now sits, a haunted

old man, lovingly clutching a porcelain jar,

the ashes of guilt that lie silently within the

walls of her urn.

Legacy

swaying erratically
as a dry-rot tree;
withering and dying,
destroying your legacy.

showing no understanding
for blood that was spilled;
never stopping to regard
the graves so many filled.

despising wise guidance
of enlightened instruction;
preferring to rush
yourselves to destruction.

From Window to Marquee

Appearing from gray shadows surrounded by

a rectangular frame, her head emerges covered

by her only brightness, a floral scarf.

Her life, overcome by green parasites, is Death

Valley, her heart is Antarctica.

Loose upper arms droop over her window sill.

Her eyes, as hungry searchlights, crawl in stealth

through the streets, whether day-busy or night-still.

Her neck cranks like a mechanical crane, in stretched

contortions. Murmurs of soft-spoken words are

amplified inside her ears like sound waves through

a tunnel; and her tongue is linen hung on clotheslines

on a gusty day. She tears secret pages from between

the covers of tightly shut books, and with spiteful

madness, disperses them through the streets where

they spin helplessly in nakedness, consumed as bits

of garbage by swine that snort for more. Soon, yawning

wounds will be exhibited on billboards. Discomfiture

will overcome minds as to how their private papers lie

exposed on sidewalks. Lives of cloistered discretions now

scream from marquees as scandal gets tangled in the brushes

of street sweepers. The window ornament's face melts into

a grotesque smile of smugness as she disappears into gray

shadows surrounded by a rectangular frame.

Theater of Lesser Value

I ran to the river for answers, but the blood-infused river only wept. I ran to the mountain for clarity,

but the mountain only showed me a wider view of my ugliness. I ran to the valley for refuge, but the valley

only moaned sad whispers. None could explain the callous theater, with plush, vicious seats that shred

dignity, until even the cords of DNA fibers were ripped thoroughly. The actors' verdict was the branding

of my guilt for being defective, condemned to a life of lesser value, imprisoned behind invisible bars

of hopelessness. I was given putrid wounds as gifts, and the audience applauded. I was twisted like glass

in fire, pressured, like forcing a circle to fit into a small square. I was the curtain rising, spread like a banner, every

part of me held up for degradation and mockery. They designated a parched place for me; and demanded I

stay there and learn to be what they wanted me to be so that I could pass the test of acceptability.

Pressed boots on my neck of humanity commanded subservient passivity and threw my wisdom to the sea. Yet no one could tell me why, no one could tell me how to calm the raging waters that

hid beneath a placid smiling lake. My inheritance was to pay for the crime and sin of emerging

from the womb with the color of my skin detested. Dispensable lives, tossed on dusty roadsides

to struggle against dying piece by piece, and taught to define as beneficent these stage actors who gave

a standing ovation to freedom, trivializing my pain. They told me to forget, and I close my eyes to erase

the agony, yet the haunts chase me, with reminders that from the first act, I was deemed

powerless in a theater I did not create, which taught me nothing as much as it taught me hate.

Shrieking Shadows

it playfully sways in
bewitching hours of
darkness within the
room's heaviness.

gaily swaggering
in the full moonlight
and shrieking winds of
the night, it throws
ghastly shapes into
obscure corners,
overpowering reason .

reaching out
to terrify, its fingers
lunge forward,
as it purrs spooky
tales of unseen spirits
or a murderous heart
hidden in the shadows.

delightfully flinging
its ghostly drama on
the wall screen, it rises
up, waving and laughing
hysterically,
again and again, until
I am compelled to stalk
to the window, closing
it sharply in indignation,

calming the mocking
curtain that teasingly
says, "What fears I can
create with wind,
darkness, and
the imagination!"

Private (Senryu)

cheerful faces laugh
while pain hides behind the eyes;
sorrow weeps inside

Beauty (Diamonte)

Beauty,
striking, radiant,
enticing, alluring, charming,
grace, pretty, repulsive, hideous,
revolting, disgusting, unappealing,
gruesome, nasty
ugliness.

The Song

Babylon, Babylon!

Living for the day, corrupt, and reckless,
You have become lawless, full, and gluttonous.
Baal, your god, has twisted your mind.
Your languid eyes are shielded and blind.

A stranger to truth
is Babylon!

Altars of might you fiercely build
While the cornerstone slips beneath your heel.
You sacrifice lives from dusk to dawn
So seeds of madness are continually spawned.

Conscience and morals perverted
in Babylon!

A deplorable assemblage slipping off the edge
Squeezing last drops of truth out of knowledge.
Snakes and scorpions are words you utter;
You pimp your whores that slither in the gutter.

Top-to-bottom justice turned backward
by Babylon!

Against oppression and inequity, to the world you rail
As you raise your money and praise to Baal
To keep him fat, deceitful, and satisfied,
So that your crafty wickedness can be justified.

Where is your god-consciousness
oh Babylon!?

You hold contempt for your own children of light,
Turn your proud ears from mouths that speak right.
Arrogance is lifted in grand licentious feasts,
Stones of hypocrisy thrown by Baal's high-priests.

Your days of grace have passed for full healing;
Instead of strutting, your legs should be kneeling
Because your scales are slanted, rickety, and reeling.

Truth and Justice are falling
with Babylon!

The Altar of Baal

Baal is a ravenous god,
thirsting for blood to keep him alive.
He commissions his high priests
to seek the souls of the weak
so that the kingdom of Babylon thrives.

I Can't Remember When

rapid powerful popping,
thumping sounds of
the heart echo
inside the ear's inner chambers,
stunning the mind.
hate soars from cold
steel, colder hearts.

piercing screech
of car tires fade into the
distance while the shrill
of the lonely siren
grows nearer.

some soul will wrestle with
death tonight—
perhaps death will win.
if there was ever a time I didn't
hear these sounds,
I can't remember when.

Song of Barking Madness

This must be a first in history's
recorded log, he says he's a man, yet
loves to call himself a dog. Sounds like
he needs a solution for his warped
self- created hybrid of confusion.

One barks at first, and then they all do;
imbeciles leading the morons, they all
crawl and fall in the doggie ditch.
Can't decide whether to walk on
four legs or two. Open their mouths
and talk that same old doggie do-do.

Now he smiles and grins at me, but
excuse me if I'm not in the mood
for one who is proud to eat dog food.
Run, dog, please scurry away;
you can ever brighten my day.

Once you see yourself as a dog, what of
intelligence do you have to say? There's
no way we can ever get hitched; we cannot
connect, because I am a woman. I am not
a bitch.

How Fast He Runs

I was stunned at how fast he moved, running and panting. I watched

as he ran past and wondered how long he would last. He ran

to the streets to meet others like himself, boys in confused lunacy

who played with toy guns that fired grown-up bullets. That stinging thud

on the back of his head, searing heat in his brain made him think that the

warnings his parents tried to give his sixteen-year old mind were true.

He would tell them that they were right if he could make it home, where

he knew he would be safe, seeing his younger brother and sister's smiles

as they watched a funny TV show. His mother would be finishing the

dinner dishes, thinking about what to wear to work tomorrow, and his

father would now be waiting for him to return from the store, except he

didn't go to the store. Instead, there was madness wrangling with folly

on dark streets. But now, overcome by an uneasy fear, he was coming

home ... running, unaware of the blood pouring down his back or the

strength of his legs melting away as a strange heaviness invaded his body.

He felt himself falling, slowly, as though he were far away. He thought he heard his mother scream his name. Calling him to get up for school. He tried to answer, but he was too sleepy. His last sensation was the gritty cold concrete of the sidewalk pressed against his face, and he couldn't understand why his bed pillow was so hard. Then he dreamt he was running again, but the door to his house began to fade. He almost made it to his home just a few yards away. Instead, he made it to the hospital DOA. Each day, so as not to disturb the dead, I carefully skipped around the trail of his darkened crimson drops, which soon disappeared into cobwebbed folders on dusty shelves.

Loving City in Blank

From where in this city comes all this bliss?
Folks are just loving each other to death.
Cherished possessions and esteemed trinkets
Are shared freely and given, by snatching.
Tender embraces, so full of joyous
Fervor ... it leaves the huggers black and blue.

Such a Beautiful Home

years evaporated into barriers against
angst, parallel lives of status mask icy
eyes behind the public smiles.
love is a shattered mirror that reflects
his splintered conscience
and fragments of broken yesterdays.

she sits, drowning in a watery glaze,
staring at faded cheerful faces locked
somewhere in time, imprisoned by
weeping picture frames as the rancid
fragrance of flowers wilted on their bed
fills the stifling room.

he stalks, as a hungry predator, deep into
the night to numb his empty wildness,
as the walls of their beautiful home creak
and sway under the burden of brittle coldness
and unbearable politeness.

S-sense

a fire called spirit
burns high
in snapping brilliance,
curls in layers
of flickers within shadows,
or warm smolders
that pierce through
walls of matter,
always fluid, soaring,
a fire called spirit
never extinguished—
no never.

Will the Real Treasure Please Stand Up?

I spoke with her just the other day,
she explained to me how they
showed her tricks to strip naked,
pose and stare into cameras on cue,
open her thighs wide and told her
to show the world her brains

She was the headline star; the men
cheered to see how far she would go,
then laughing, they jeered and called

her a ho as she showed the world
her self-worth. She jiggled, shook it,
wiggled and dropped it: squatted
and lifted her leg, her best sexual
antics performed to make them beg.

She forgot the fears she carried,
carved deep inside her mind,
the bruised bits of reality whispered
that her only power was her
game of provocative seduction
and her ability to make the men want her.

Enablers were clever enough
with their constant chant they told
enticing tales to her hungry ears
about how perfectly beautiful
her body was, their cut-out

doll to acquiesce and show
the world that a piece of meat
was the thing she was born to be.
So she would grind it, back it up,
be the obedient little girl

and pop out the tits for all to see;
lolled on the pages of a magazine,
while the shadowy pimps who call
themselves respectable businessmen
molded her to show the world
her best notion of dignity.

She was the willing pawn in her own
self-degradation when the dollar
sign was lifted high for female exploitation.
Her mind screamed in anger as
she clawed at the ground and buried

her real treasure there, wasted
away, unpolished and useless,
as she told herself that it was okay
to accept the worst of lies.

Smoke Screams*

One day in my neighborhood
I saw a bomb drop
Trembles reverberated
As houses shook and rocked

An intense fire blasted
The inferno's heat churned
Police and firemen stood by
To watch the destruction burn

When the fire completed its ruin
The results left eyes in shock
It extinguished adults and children
And destroyed two city blocks

Melted light poles, charred trees
Cindering homes of memories
Engulfed in dense black smoke
Incinerated in a senseless tragedy

But by far, much worse
Than destroyed properties
Were lives wrapped in body bags
Snuffed out unnecessarily

High city officials proclaimed
Intention didn't cause all this harm
And that there was no crime committed
Brushing it off like a fly on the arm

History records another mockery made
Of freedom and democracy
A punitive action delivered
To those who protested inequality

These same city officials
Hid their hands, denied they lied
Connived to give sane explanations
For the day justice died

*MOVE Bombing. May 1985

God's Managers

the created marionette dances
to the tune of confused folly
controlled by skillful hands
made to bow to mundane demands.

tucked neatly in worn pockets
or faithfully carried around,
sometimes abandoned in orderly
closets until convenience takes
it down from the shelf, when the self,
in despair, falls into cavernous ground.

when the conscience, frozen in midnight,
stretches between wrong and right,
the divine puppet is molded
and pressed to acquiesce,
bowing to our whims in flight
and to the smug bigotry to which we cling,
slyly obscured in pretty boxes
tied with colorful string.

to illuminate numerous layers
of our cryptic souls, we do not dare.
we shield our hearts from answers
and unknown haunts that lurk there,
treading softly on doubt
so as not to shatter platitudes of faith,
keeping God manageable
and religion easy to bear.

The Comedy of Change

They trot on the high road,
crawl on the low road,
struggle to balance the center load
while the left is left hanging and
the right drinks tea
of lunatic madness.
The money controllers
revel in gladness, and those in the middle,
not knowing where to go,
are dangling
from a cliff over the rocky ravine
below …
all because change
means more of the same
remains unchanged.

Sleep (Senryu)

tired denizens
weary of the same old lies
simmer in their sleep.

Hidden (Senryu)

it's the hairline cracks
trickling with threads of water
that sink mighty ships.

No Thinking Allowed Song

They tell you stupid
And teach minds dumb
Steal you from real
Until conscience is numb

They grasp you down
To where you never been
Just try to climb up
They pull you down again

They break your spirit
And say it is your fault
Because you wouldn't feast
On the lies they taught

They want to make you
What you don't want to be
Deceive your inner sight
So that you cannot see

They walk in rotten
And teeth smile pretend
They want to take you
To hell with them

Thinking: Login attempt failed
Access denied

An Epitaph

lust esteemed
on thrones of desire.
hot bodies prance
to stoke the fire.
unfilled craving
a dance cold-hearted;
here lies the despised
gems of real love,
the dearly departed.

Subway

When did the child spirit die;
or perhaps it was still alive
lost beyond the horizon
chasing rainbows of promise
that disappear too quickly.
Did we ever know
the effervescent ecstasy of joy
or the peace of a simple life?

As I study faces reflected
 in smudged windows,
images shackled by
the hardness of misery,
our eyes stare into vacant
shadows of defeat,

shoulders slumped in tiredness,
pulled down by the weight
of thick blurry thoughts, we roll
through time on littered

speeding trains inside the city's
damp and dark tunnels
of gray mildewed reality.

A Peculiar Word

Have you heard?
It's time to sharpen
your scalpel
when they pin on the label
"controversial"
because it usually means
that you're cutting
close to a nerve.

The Searching Sack

Some might think it hilarious;
others say it's some kind
of eccentric madness,
but I always carry a sack

containing a microscope, a
huge magnifying glass,
and digging tools; and like
an archeologist or anthropologist,

I search diligently, digging
for any and all
miniscule and microscopic
particles of justice.

A Good Day for Shopping

This will be the last time he leaves her,
he yelled, slamming the door in anger.
 She didn't care that he preferred the
other, and his dramatics made her laugh.
She smoothed out a piece of paper
to write her shopping list so as not
to take his expected departure too hard;
after all, she had what she wanted
as she hastily headed for the door
with his pin number and bank card.

A Pandemic of Hate

it sashays boldly
a shameless swagger
through the earth
it is thick green pus
foul and oozing
from an infectious disease
it proudly proclaims it name
empty of remorse
spreading its pandemic
contagious
sickness of the mind.

Control Numbers

Humans, shredded in
the clutches of numbers,
hemorrhage throughout
society. Their lives, dreams,
dignity less important than
the blistering iron brand
of the numbers
that define and bind them.

The Story of Eyes

Crusty old thoughts
shrunken inside

innocent-looking shells
of hate lie in wait

to twist tongues into
lashing what's different.

Some yell loudly,
louder than the mind

needs to hear; some
whisper softly when

they think no one is near.
Others neither yell

nor whisper; their eyes
tell the whole story.

Closeness

she could not bear
to remove her apron
so she tied its strings
around their necks
like a noose and pulled
tightly, with skill,
so as not to kill
but just enough
to keep them
dangling near.

Sliding

a terrifying boulder grows larger,
only one step behind, its shadow
pressing down hard on my
spirit. my feet slide low,
cutting against sharp
rocks, into stagnant
quicksand; but I
hold on to an
unraveling cord
called hope,
praying it
doesn't
snap
today.

Shut

this
thing
called love
has become a
prowling specter
carrying pain from
the past. Trust makes
itself difficult to find. when
the yearning heart says
open, the doors quickly
shut, closed by the
teardrop of a
suspicious
mind.

Climb and Pull

Don't expect it
to be placed in

your lap.
Softly knock

on the door,
lounge around,

or go sauntering by.
If you really

want it,
must have it,

climb over hell,
reach up, and

pull heaven down
from the sky.

Poem Interview

Did you tell a story?
"No."

Speak of ancient history and glory?
"No."

Preach a timely message?
"No."

Impart mystical hidden knowledge?
"No."

Tell of passion and devotion?
"No."

Set hearts and minds in motion?
"Yes,
now you are beginning
to understand my secret potion."

Humorology

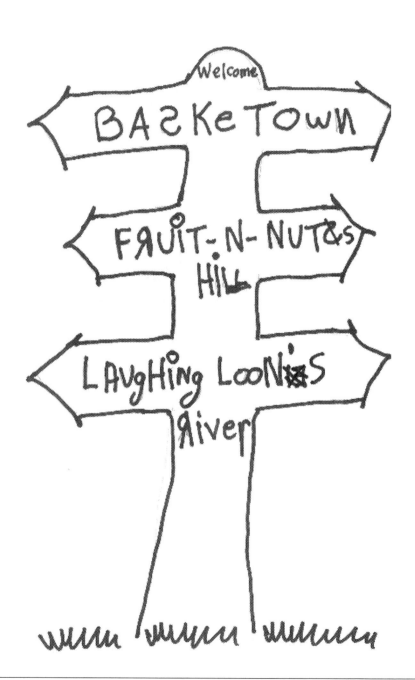

Welcome to Basketown

There was once an obscure little place called Basketown,
though on the average map it couldn't be found.

On its north boundary was Fruit-n-Nuts Hill,
on its southern border was the famous Basketown Mill.

Two long rivers ran on its borders east and west—
the Laughing Loons River and the River Joke-n-Jest.

Now, Basketown did well, surviving on its own.
Many just passing through made it their permanent home.

The Basketown people were happy, and the friendliest;
they held great admiration for each other's weirdness.

The townsfolk held important meetings from time to time
to create their poems, even though they forced the rhymes.

Outsiders said Basketown was a strange community,
but the townsfolk understood each other's peculiarities.

The townspeople lived ordinary lives like you or me,
except they spent a lot of time laughing hysterically.

They held elections, bake sales, parades, and bazaars,
had TVs, computers, and drove around in beat-up cars.

The town had famous monuments, theaters, and sports,
tourist attractions, malls, and vacation resorts.

See, the townspeople were folks who thought life was funny;
they didn't care for status, rules, clocks, or money.

Sometimes, for no reason, they would just jump and shout,
run around in circles, and let it all hang out!

They whistled through their days without much of a care,
each one mumbling, laughing, and talking to no one there.

The townsfolk loved to have visitors or tourists around,
so they crooned this tune called "The Basketown Sound."

"Visit Basketown! Its sights and people will make you smile.
Who knows? perhaps you'll settle in and stay for a while!"

The Townspeople: Daisy and Lee

There was once a happy lady named Daisy.
All the townspeople said she was crazy.

She talked very loud and shouted with glee
to her loyal imaginary friend she called Lee.

Daisy said she and Lee danced a jazzy jitterbug;
and they always shared the same whiskey jug.

With Lee, Daisy was always grinning and carefree
though this friend called Lee, no one else could see.

Now, Daisy was humongous, round, and fat;
she squeezed into her clothes, and even her hats!

At the town fair, Daisy piled two plates with food.
She ate every bit, thinking, *To leave food is so rude.*

The townsfolk said, "Two plates of food is too much!"
But Daisy replied, "Your mouths you should hush,

I really don't eat too much, you see.
I only ate one plate ... the other was eaten by Lee!"

The Townspeople: Honeychile

The townspeople called her Honeychile.
She was flamboyant, loose, and wild.
She painted her door red,
Sprinkled roses on her bed.
All the fellas left her house with a smile.

The Townspeople: Ol' Liza

The townspeople called her Ol' Liza.
She said, "I'm-ah gifted, psychic, and ah-wise-ah."
She would stare, chant, and call
Into her huge crystal ball,
Saying, "The spirits need ah-money to ah-guide ya."

The Townspeople: Jack Hats

The townspeople called him Jack Hats.
He wore hats that represented this and that.
He was the town sheriff, judge, and baker,
notary public, butcher, and undertaker!
But Jack didn't mind; he liked being busy.
He rushed here and there, aimlessly, daily,
yet always remained calm, pleasant, and friendly.
Jack said he could keep it all under control.
He managed well—until one day, I was told:
he arrested himself, and cut the fat from his toes,
set the prisoners free and notarized his nose;
while eulogizing a funeral of a dear one who died,
Jack put on a birthday hat and sang "Here Comes the Bride!"

The Townspeople: Fred

He was a visitor named bigoted Fred.
His face was like pie dough and his neck was red.
He never dug a ditch
Because he was born rich;
He swaggered with a buzzard's shit nest on his head!

The Townspeople: Sue Sideshow

The townsfolk called her Sue Sideshow Tragedy.
She wore a B cup, but wanted to wear double E.
She had an enhancement operation
But to the townsfolk's consternation,
She now hops through the streets topless for all to see!

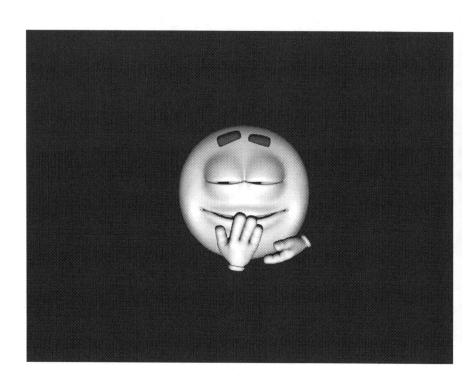

The Townspeople: Dr. Slicker

There was once a psychiatrist named Dr. Slicker.
Unfortunately, all of his patients became sicker.

So his patients had a meeting, deciding together
To take Dr. slicker to the Laughing Loons River.

Once there, they hanged him upside-down from a tree,
And then took turns tickling his feet mercilessly.

Confessing, Dr. Slicker laughed, saying, "Stop! no more,
I admit it ... I bought my medical license from the dollar store!"

The Townspeople: Cye

There was once an old woman named Cye.
She was mean, conniving, and sly.
She would sit on her stoop,
And throw a pail of poop
On anyone who happened to pass by!

The Townspeople: Mr. Clyde

The townspeople called him Aged Mr. Clyde.
After fifty-five years of marriage, his wife died.
When they married, she was such a young bride.
At her funeral, poor Clyde cried and bawled.
At the burial, her name Clyde sorrowfully called.
He made such a heart-wrenching, grievous scene—
The next day, he had a new bride who was only sixteen!

The Townspeople: Vanishing Kay

The townsfolk called her Vanishing Kay.
She was skinny but thought she was fat anyway.
Good food ... she wouldn't buy it
Because she was always on a diet.
One day the wind blew and carried her away!

The Townspeople: Wild Bill

The townspeople called him Wild Bill.
He lived right beside Fruit-n-Nuts Hill.

He wore cowboy boots and cowboy hats
And spent his nights shooting at muskrats.

Every Tuesday morning at ten o'clock
He would try to sell folks his painted rocks.

Wild Bill and his hogs drank spiked eggnog,
And then would spend the day playing wild leap-frog!

If the hogs won by scoring the most points,
Poor Wild Bill would sob, "Oink, oink oink!"

The Townspeople: Round Peg

The townspeople called her Round Peg.
She was hefty and wore a wooden leg.
She hobbled and hopped,
But a wooden leg could not stop
The unstoppable peg-leg Round Peg.

The Townspeople: Rosy

The Townspeople called her Nosy Rosy.
She spied while hiding behind bushes and posies.
She spent all her time playing sleuth.
She slanted and dramatized the truth,
Turned folk's private lives into outlandish stories!

The Townspeople: Mr. Wind

The townsfolk called him Mr. Con-Man Wind.
They bolted their doors so he couldn't get in.
He tried to beguile
With his shivering smile,
And peered through windows with a frosty grin.

The Townspeople: Jittery Englebout

The townspeople called him shaky J. Englebout.
He hid in his house, afraid to come out.
He feared his shadow or the shadow of a mouse.
If someone knocked at the door, he ran behind the couch.
J. Englebout was jittery, so much his body shook,
And his coffee mugs fell from the nook's wall hooks!
J. Englebout chewed the nails from his fingers,
His toes too; then he started chewing his furniture!
The townsfolk said "socializing" was what he needed
So, "Come to the town fair!" they begged and pleaded.
To miss the town fair, well, Englebout wouldn't dare
Besides, he wanted those townspeople out of his hair.
So Englebout decided to go to the town fair.
Once there, he trembled and thought they all stared.
Halfway through the festivities, in anguished despair,
The townsfolk begged Englebout to leave the Town Fair
When he started chewing up the bandstand, tables, and chairs!

The Townspeople: Mr. I. N. DeGrass

The townsfolk called him Rambling In DeGrass
He searched for himself by taking a daily psych class.
Folks said, "To escape your rut,
Go find yourself in your butt,"
Now he rolls around town with his head in his ass!

The Townspeople: The Merry Moores

There was once a couple called the Merry Moores.
They had children: Cal, Jill, Hal, John, and Lenore,
Sue, Ray, Jay, Ben, and Egor,
May, Jim, Lou, Sal, Drew, and Eleanor,
And a new baby they couldn't think of a name for!

The Townspeople: Babby Boohoo

The townsfolk called her Bah-Bah Babby Boohoo.
She would purposefully fall, and then she would sue.
One day she fell on her head,
Now she can't get out of bed.
Her hubby took her settlement and fled to Honolulu!

The Townspeople: Mr. Hagawath

The townspeople called him Mr. Hagawath.
He didn't like soap and never took a bath.
His long, shaggy hair made children fear him.
He smelled so badly, no one could get near him.

When Hagawath walked by, flowers would die
And barnyard animals hung their heads and cried
"Mr. Hagawath, go take the bath you never had.
Don't come near us because you smell too bad!"

Well, the townsfolk met with Mr. Hagawath one day,
And with clothespins on their noses, I heard them say,
"Mr. Hagawath, you are running the tourists away!"
But Mr. Hagawath replied, "If you don't like the way I smell,

Then all you townspeople can just go to hell!"
So the townsfolk dragged him to the River Joke-n-Jest,
To give Mr. Hagawath a lesson on cleanliness.
Well, Hagawath was angry; he cussed and screamed.

The townsfolk said, "We're not trying to be mean."
And with lye soap, they scrubbed him until he was clean.
They washed Hagawath's hair and gave him a manicure,
Brushed his teeth, and then finished with a pedicure.

He was primped, picked, combed, powdered and fluffed,
Then deodorized, dunked, perfumed, shined and buffed.
After Mr. Hagawath was clean, he looked very his best.
When the dirt came off, he weighed ten pounds less!

The Townspeople: Ms. Down

The townspeople called her Ms. Right-Side Down.
She drank hallucinatory tea and wanted to rule the town.

She used homespun talk as though raised on a farm.
To remember her name, she had to write it on her arm.

She had a shrill voice, but that was no deterrent
To her silly speeches that were always incoherent.

The townsfolk used tape so that her mouth was bound,
Saying, "You're so weird that even *we* don't want you around!"

The Townspeople: Lazy Nick

The townspeople called him Lazy Nick.
He spent his days watching prick and chick flicks.
The townsfolk were appalled
When he wandered through the mall,
Beating his dick with a stick!

The Townspeople: Ms. Sighter

The townspeople called her Ms. Word Sighter.
She wore crumpled papers and said she was a writer.
Blank pages made her uptighter.
She had red eyes from writing all nighters.
In the mornings, her mirror couldn't stand the sight of her!

The Townspeople: Mr. Newspaper Ned

The townspeople called him Mr. Newspaper Ned
He ran the town tabloid, and this is what he said:
Aliens had taken over his backyard.
The healthiest food to eat is lard.
His male dog just gave birth to monkeys under his bed!

The Townspeople: Ms. Hawkings

The townspeople called her Ms. Phone Hawkings.
On the phone she was always whining and squawking.
Folks would wax their floors,
Go shopping at the store,
Come back to their phone, and she was still talking!

Basketown: The End

So now you've met a few good folks who live in Basketown.
They're all still there (though Fred is confined to the dog pound!)

And Kay, after the wind blew her away so easily,
Became entangled in the branch of a toasted nuts tree.

She now has a new job, much to her delight:
She lets the town kids fly her around like a kite.

That poor Ms. Down was rushed out of town with a shiver
After the townspeople threw her in the Laughing Loons River!

Basketown even has a brand-new botanical zoo,
Though many townsfolk decided to live in it too.

They built a new city hall, south of the River Joke-n-Jest;
And hired sloofy clowns to run the government offices.

So come by the town sometime for a free buffet lunch,
Of nutty soup, flakey biscuits, and fruity fruit punch.

Many new people have settled there to live,
Enjoying weird smiles that only Basketown can give.

THE END

It Survived

Somehow, it survived
The poem was determined to stay alive,
Even though it suffered abuse
From adverb, adjective
And punctuation overuse.

A Cat Wears Its At (Out)

I saw a tomcat, proud and fat,
it wore a sun hat to hide the fact
that its pudgy head was flat.
It fiercely guarded its habitat
and strutted around like an aristocrat.
It winked at me, ready to act,
jumped in midair like an acrobat,
and nabbed a gnat with a quick paw pat,
then suddenly grabbed a baseball bat
to chase and hiss at a startled rat,
which didn't have much time to react.
So the robust zoomfastic fat cat
caught it for lunch, belched, then sat on a mat.
It stuck out its chest and readjusted its hat,
smiled at me and yawned, ready to chat,
and said, "Can *you* top that?"

Party Animal or Party Soaker?

We danced last night hard and hearty!
Really knew how to turn up the party.
Grabbed our fill of food, drinks, and laughs-
Ah ... today we must soak in Epsom Salts baths!

The Elusive Feat

I can lift the heaviest weights
And sleep on a bed of nails.
Walking through fire is an easy task.
I can make the heavens rain hail!

I can swallow the longest sword
Or cause a mean bear to run away.
Bend a spoon with only a stare
And walk on water any day!

All these feats I can easily do
(and many more than these go untold).
Oh how I wish I only knew
How to keep my weight under control!

Silly Song of the Black Cat and 13

Greenish eyes glittered
slyly in the night.
Eyes without a body,
what an eerie sight!

Thirteen thrilling shivers
filled my gut with dread.
Thirteen chilling hairs
stood up on my head!

The greenish eyes flashed
a light of thirteen beams,
fading 'til no longer seen!
This is my thirteen-line rhyme
of the black cat and thirteen.

A Little Wiggle

I will dance a little wiggle for you
If you wiggle a little dance for me.
With all our dancing
And endless prancing
We will make two wiggles become three.

Change Subject

When I told people I was writing a book,
They gazed at me with an unbelieving look.
Said, "Well, we have a bridge for sale too,"
Changed the subject, saying, "So what else is new?"

Bills (Tetracys)

life
must be
nothing more
than paying bills,
so my mail slot tells me from day to day.

It's That Witch!

her green face and cackles
caused nightmares in the night
the tall, black pointy hat
gave my child's mind such a fright.

i feared she'd come and beat me
snatch me from my room
just like that hairy little doggie
she'd fly me on her broom.

i would run and hide in closets
or crawl beneath the bed
visions of her hour glass
wreaked havoc in my head.

nightmares from a while ago
those innocent childhood fears
her sneers and blackened fingernails
would fade throughout the years.

so you can understand the shock
when one day i turned on my TV
and there she was pointing at me
and trying to sell me coffee!

she no longer wore the pointy hat
but in my memories i knew
her new disguise couldn't fool me
and i'd never drink that witch's brew!

Essay on Poetry and Birdcages

1
Sitting here being introspective
about my humble attempts at poetry,
a personal perspective; although
I am probably not very objective. I
am told not to use too much
rhyme, within sentences or on the
end of my poems' lines. However,
my rhymes on lines are not done
deliberately. I let the words unfold
with their own spontaneity, hopefully
to communicate with readers simply,
and plainly. To rhyme or not to rhyme,
I cannot answer that question. Words
have a way of forming on the paper
in their own positions.

2
Thinking along further, I have to
confess, even though I know a little
about writing, I probably know less
concerning forms of blank verse,
traditional, or lyrical, prose, free verse,
avant-garde, or satirical. All I know
is that writing, to me, is purely medicinal.
Critics have said, "Go take a poetry
Class," and one day I might; but I
am afraid I wouldn't pass, because
sitting in those hard chairs is an aching
pain in my ass.

3
Once, I read some poems, and then
afterward became angry, because I could
not understand what the poet was saying.
I skipped past the poem in an indignant
huff and thought, *Well maybe that poem*
is too deep or my mind just isn't
deep enough.

4
However, reflecting further over those
poems, feeling a bit confused, to myself
I mused: *Why would a poet write out*
lines to share that only he/she understands?
To the reader, this isn't fair, besides, I
grow weary of reading poems that make
me want to pull out my hair! Well,
I guess all poets are guilty of occasionally
going to the extreme of pushing the
metaphors over the cliff into abstract,
ambiguous, lofty lines. I just don't think
that a poet should do it all the time.
Writing poetry where the idea fails to
communicate … well, I don't understand the
reasons, except that there's a thin line
between creative art and egotistical delusions.

5
So, personally speaking, just between you
and me, for readers to understand and enjoy
poetry, they shouldn't have to go to a leading
university and take a three hundred dollar
course called something like Poetry 101:
Dissecting and Deconstructing the Metaphorical
Chemistry of Poetry Scientifically!

6

This brings me to the end of my poetry "essay."
If you're still reading, I'm glad you decided to
stay. If you read any of my poems that are too
boring, too high, or too deep to communicate,
but instead begin to irritate and your senses,
frustrate, please don't fly into an exasperated
rage. I wouldn't want you to waste your
money, because my poems might come in
handy for some other purpose ... perhaps to
line someone's birdcage? You can believe my
words; I would not think it absurd, because
I like birds.

Water Visions

Simply Moon

Moonlight rising
as silhouettes on the sun.

Moon rays glowing,
time's yesterday is done.

Moonbeams dropping
on waves of radiant sea.

Moon force calling,
"earth waters, dance for me."

Visitation of the Gnomes

Familiar gloom seizes my mind.
My ears detect a foreboding sound.
A mob of numerous hammering hands
In a frenzy, loudly thump and pound.

I feel their impish marching feet
Sprint on the rooftop of my home.
I know the feverish busy schemes
Of those mischievous gnomes.

They gurgle, spit, and whisper giggles.
Tools chisel with rhythmic taps.
Laughter rises to a merry crescendo
Overflowing with those naughty claps.

The squeaky voices mock and taunt.
Resounding echoes bounce in the hall.
Still, determined, they drop in uninvited.
Clumsily, they slide down the walls.

Watching imps dance on misty windows,
Their liquid silhouettes swagger and streak,
I remember I used to love a rainy day
That is … until my roof began to leak.

Deep Well

My well was hidden
beneath calcified
stones and weeds
of tangled straw.

My well appeared
voluminous, layers of
shadows intertwined
with dim light.

I lowered myself
inside, sliding into
gray, musty clamminess.

all this effort
just to search
find even one
drop of forgiveness.

Inside (Senryu)

Glance, unassuming
at the exterior walls,
peer hard through windows.

Sand (Diamonte)

Sand,
grainy, hot,
burning, searing, scorching,
powder, grit, stream, brook,
sparkling, cleansing, soothing,
cool, turquoise
water.

Disconnected

surrounded by hordes
of faces, I watch
a raging swirl,
the feeding frenzy,
agitated nerves,
listen to the shrill
pitch and low grumbles,
feel the dramas
and try not
to get a headache.

I crave isolation.

The Ache of Desire

dried with ashen cracks
the dusty vase
yearns in thirst
consumed by internal flames,
murmurs prayers to be
absorbed in,

and filled by
eternal ethereal waters
to bathe the searing heart,

uniting a soul's wanderings
with the Infinite's Oneness.

the ache of longing
to rest inside the
fountain of divine timelessness,
drinking liquid crystal
from a gold goblet,
where peace is
a constant state of being,
the jeweled crown
of all blessings.

Whoever Said?

I hid inside trembles
but it found me anyway
so I ran, but it chased me
without abating. I stopped
running because I had enough.
I stood tough to face it
eye-to-eye, nose-to-nose
my fiercest pose
without swaying.
it punched me like a prizefighter,
pummeled me like putty
pressed into the ground,
left me with scarred knees,
scraped elbows, gasping for air
twigs stuck in my hair,
a bruised butt
and bells in my ears.
whoever it was who said
we should face our fears
never met mine.

Oasis

love, a murky pool of
quicksand, sits grinning
concealed beneath
the oasis of a pure
serene lake,
waiting for the
spellbound to jump in.

Splattering

Make words tip-toe
softly?
No,
but as a thunderous
waterfall, rolling
and tumbling,
gushing forth,
rushing energy,
bursting flashes,
water chasing
water, surging
in abandonment,

fling the words high!
Let them unfurl
and twirl
freely,
splashing, spilling
like brilliant colors
falling, sweeping,
splattering
on paper canvas,
writing a portrait.

Though We Stumble

Better to be dead
Buried in the grave
Than to be living
Numb on the inside instead,
As decay.

Better to search for
Passions of life not found
Than to wither away
Into a dry, fruitless ground,
Today.

Better to grasp for
Truth and fight confusion
Than to embrace life
In a lucid delusion,
Astray.

Better to keep on,
Though we stumble and grope,
Than to accept the fate
Of life without hope,
I pray.

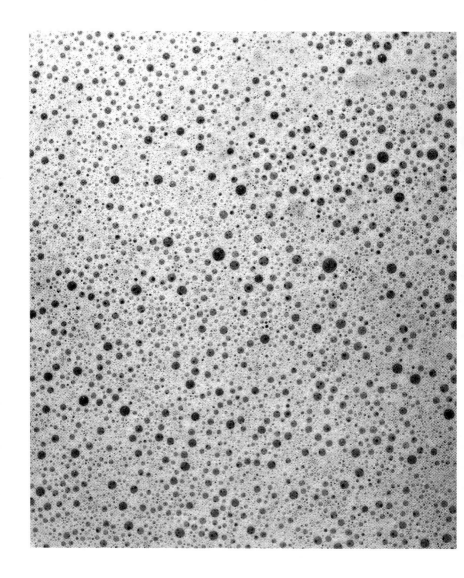

Sanity Like Soapy Water

I stared at the sink and watched sanity slowly
disappear, just like the soapy water, spinning
reckless currents into the porcelain's frothing mouth:

bright yellow beams sparkle
and reflect the light inside
engraved patterns of stemware
filled with happy bubbles of sweet
intoxicating crude.
clinking bells echo softly as glasses
are raised in triumph, hands
shake hands in jubilation.
contracts are hurriedly written
signed in ink made of human blood.
history is sickened once again,
truth crushed into unbreakable top
level secrets, sealed within
the darkness of flag-draped coffins,
classified information buried in
uncountable, insignificant sandy graves;
and humanity submits to its
grandiose delusions of fear, refusing
to hear the subtle sounds of cracking.

the residue of water swirls round and round,
trickles down the drain until the last soapy bubble
bursts, leaving an empty sink full of questions.
And I vomit.

How Long?

I hear
they say
all will
be okay
when morning
comes
and night
has passed,
but never
a word
spoken about
how long
a night
can last.

Before Walking

I heard
the talk
about how
we must
crawl before
we walk,
but they didn't
tell it all
about how
we must
grovel before
we crawl.

Love Beginnings

can the mind hear it?
what's that sound?
hearts thumping
doing the rhumba,
drums pumping
riding high
in bliss that's
rising unbound
inside stirrings
of dizzy magic
spinning around.
cracks become
openings, breaking
down the wall.
hearts slipping
unguarded,
sliding, tripping
about to fall.

Ripples of Faith

My spirit
is armor, scratched,
dented with chinks
but still shining.

My heart
is rubber, bounced
against walls, bruised
yet still pliable.

My hope
is a buoy, tossed
into windswept waters
but still afloat.

My faith
is glass, chipped
edges jagged, cracked
though not broken.

My soul
is paper, scribbled
upon and crumpled
yet not torn apart.

My vision
is fire, smoldering
cinders, a flickering
flame not out.

My spirit
is a mirror, smudged
but absorbing and reflecting
gleams of light.

Coming To Terms

I dreamed he was lying down,
His breathing had ceased, and then
He was breathing again.
In waking grogginess
I could not remember
If he was dead or alive.
After a moment, it became clear;
Several days ago
He had died.
The sun was rising.
Again, I cried.

Write (Tetracys)

Ears
close when
I try to
speak, so I write
my words down plainly on paper instead.

Seeker

I searched the eastern horizon
travelled the western edge
climbed a pole to the north
and dug to southern depths

still determined
I rocketed into the cosmos
swam through ocean's silence
what I sought was elusive

exhausted, I sat in dismay
that's when I found it
a tiny pearl, here all this time
inside, looking for me

Start Stopping

when you start
believing you must tuck
your dusty dreams
upon the shelf,
it is time
to stop believing
the things
you tell yourself.

Waves

a word,
travels
as energy.
it ebbs and flows
wherever it goes—
here and there
heard by ears
and seen by
whose eyes?
who knows?
the unseen
that grows.

Stillness

you are
a pond of
peace, blocking
out clatter of have-to,
must-do, run fast, outlast,
get past, push
through.
a quiet sanctuary calls
to you in whispers, to
flow with time that's
only measured by coral pebbles
resting in crystal
jade liquid.
you are
a pond of peace,
tender waters rolling,
soothing within
streams
of silence.

Of Origins

sleep
sweet release
my spirit travels
free in peace
seeing, hearing, knowing
when I awaken
little remains
of sleep's memory
except the poem's
whispers
waiting for me

Cool (Tetractys)

ride
on cool,
he said. to
ride like hothead
will do nothing for you but get you dead.

In Fear and Faith

i sit on a tree branch
that trembles
suspended in midair.
i pick green leaves
and cover them with my

heart and soul,
for reasons only
known by eternity.
yesterday cannot be
touched; tomorrow
hasn't given its gift yet.

i sit on a tree branch,
in waves of wind
perched between
fear and faith.

in fear, because this branch
might break, throwing
me into unknown
catastrophe, the ground
below as hard and cold
as humiliation
with a snarling face.

in faith, because i keep
sitting on this trembling
tree branch, anyway.

Journeys

floating on various hues
of light, they journey
back and forth over the
oceanic gulf between
states of being.
souls of birth propelled
into seasons and reasons.
the seasons are written
in mysteries of time.
the reasons are our
challenge to find.

Soft Libations

white crystal fringes
in a vertical dance
melt on the ground
racing in swirls
busy with calm intensity.
the streets are a light
covered by a darkened
glass that reflect a milky-gray
fogginess.
above, a smoky-
colored herd of buffalo
meanders across the sky,
leaving dark purple trails,
a herd so numerous that
even the sun steps aside to
let them pass.
the aroma of blossoms' dew,
a fragrance to be tasted,
drips from saturated
leaves dressed
in liquid silver.
a trancelike sedation fills
misty air as sounds of
being gently carried in
the womb whisper inside
hums of the wind.

Flashes of Serendipity

With trepidation I dive
into this mysterious sea;
surrendering to undercurrents,
swirling ripples pull me
further into its abyss.

Immersed in timelessness
where reality's beginnings
merge with dreams' endings.

As the world's clamor
melts into muffled silence,
my mind drowns in blurred
flashes of serendipity.

Watery shadows, revealed
as inner portals of light
upon which I helplessly float,
open treasures once concealed.

Gliding and sinking deeper
into unknown blurry dimensions,
I mistakenly surmised that I
was writing poetry,

yet despite my best intentions,
I was surprised to discover
that poetry was writing me.

Air Lights

A Better Kind of Madness

just me
I want to be
no need for apology
exhilarating
cool wind opens
my lungs like a curtain
and greets each pore
with shivering tingles
as the sun wraps
my head in
golden sashes
until the depths
of my spirit sprays
like a geyser, laughing
in jubilant madness.
soaring
overflowing
unrestrained
sweet madness.
I reach out, stretch to sky
firm I stand
gazing upon
the whole world
here, in
my hand.

It Vanishes

As a luminous butterfly
displays delicate energy
in a circular dance,
its antics soon carried away
upon the breeze,

Or cool water held tightly
in cupped hands, yet
still seeping through fingers
before the dry
throat is soothed,

Joy, like an ethereal spirit
which airily floats
in subtle shimmers, seen
but refusing to be
held, vanishes.

Endless Shades of Blue

A violet velvet mystery
Embroidered with pulsating gems
Displays a glimpse of eternity.
A pearl shows its royal diadems.

Amethyst canopy commands
Night visions of contemplation
As earthly consciousness expands
Across blue topaz meditation.

Jewels on indigo inspire awe.
Purple aura encompasses sleep
Anchored by divine cosmic law
As immense as the soul is deep.

Atmosphere

She interrupts with
the power of an assault
carrying the same familiar
bucket-load of jangling
chimes, downward utterances,
whining scrapes, tapping
drips, like sandpaper rubbing
silk. Her hundred and ten
dramatic dilemmas, all rolled into
minutes that are like grains
 in slow-motion
slipping through the hour
glass. As she drains oxygen
from the air, one is overcome
with a fierce need to
scream into the atmosphere
for mercy, begging
for just a little relief
from the torture.

Wings (Than-bauk)

young birds in nest
grow and rest, soon
will test their wings.

Closets (Senryu)

love wraps with arms like
a quilt of comfort and light,
opening closets.

Saxophone Tones

the jazz king
makes his sax moan
and sing musical notes
that float into passionate
elusive sounds swirling around
like March winds, or tip-toeing as
a May breeze, telling a story with melodious
beats, maybe sassy, maybe sweet, creating
notes of all hues singing melancholy
blues or ecstasy subdued. The jazz
king makes his sax sing about
heat and sweat lingering in
smoky cafes, steaming, or
a butterfly's dancing
serenade on a June
day, fluttering
carefree.

Let the Trains Roll By

today this soft bed will be
my armor, this spongy quilt
my shield from the world
out there

speeding by like a daunting
conundrum of steel,
yellow sparks spitting
from metal wheels,
propelling itself forward
only to repeat the same
journeys; its horn is
a lion's roar, pulverizing
the silence, leaving
it dazed and shaken, but

today my mind will remain
one with the refuge of this
heavenly pillow.

Arrayed

each
in their place
every space exuding
its own expression
knowing of old
young fascination
shape, form
tone unique airy light
or heavy mystique
anger, joy
elusive wonder
love, longing, and
thoughts to ponder

threads reach out
or deep within
dressing pages
again and again
in majestic tapestry
or cotton array
woven with wisdom
or naiveté
in a solitary room
of simplicity
strokes on pages
is what you see
unlocking their
sublime mystery.

What If?

see
magnificent
stars
encircling a
silver
crescent in
the sky.

"what if?"
they say
as
they feed
you
tiny drops
that
glimmer
with possibilities.

Poem's Hoax

why did you run away
with the light?
like a hoax in flight,
my heart sprinted inside
your footsteps.
I reached for you.
my pen's trap was sneaky
and snickered but you
were quicker as I watched
you quiver then crumble
like a building
imploding.
your skin shed itself
and evaporated into
a never was, a naughty
mischief, leaving my eyes
to grapple and grieve
over subtle shadows,
musty perfume
hidden without meaning,
the silence of your
nothing words
that poured tears inside,
because folks saw the
worst in me and said
that's damn good poetry.

Honeyfruit Orbits

Come, reach out, take my hand
Mystical quartz flows in this land
Honeyfruit grows on a healing tree
Essence is not confined to this galaxy

Come, get ready, glide with me
Ascend through the universe of ecstasy
Leaving behind the world's pretensions
Engulfed in orbits of love's dimensions

Cycles

today
is the day
that was once
light years away,
and tomorrow, which
we cannot see, wasn't meant
to last, for it shall soon be light years in the past.

Kingdom of the Alienated Forest

There was a time of light years in the distance of space, a place
in another celestial existence called a galaxy.
Here existed

an opulent forest shimmering green, flowing with strong
thick trees. This kingdom strained itself to evolve, like a
woman in difficult birth;

and every tree drank from its own river of wisdom. Therefore,
the forest widened its girth. In the center of the forest
was the tallest and most

mesmerizing tree, with branches long and wide. Its brilliance
could be seen for miles and from all sides. This tree was
submerged in a sparkling

light that wasn't a light. And what kind of light was this?
It was a light so dazzling it could blind the mind, seduce the
five senses, but could not give

illumination to the soul. Its branches stretched throughout
the forest, intertwining with branches of other trees. Some
tree branches it supported,

some it strangled and distorted, others it broke in half. The tall,
beautiful tree's branches were strong but weak. How could
they be strong yet weak? The outer

shell was iron, but inwardly it was weedy with its fibers
of life choked. This tall tree overflowed with sap as pleasant
as honey, intoxicating

as opium. Like other trees, its roots grew deep into the bloody soil of martyrs, and its gentle rains were the tears of its victims that poured with melodic

refrains and waited for vindication in the courts of galactic magistrates, whose eyes would frequently circulate above the forest. In haziness, beyond

layers of hills, though not quite clear, a stranger appeared as a speck on the golden horizon. He steps were very deliberate because he walked inside

cycles, each pace a mathematical equation. His eyes, more powerful than gamma rays. He trod above the constellation Virgo, and Orion's Belt was his

headband. He was the scientist of scientists and the mixer of all chemical elements. With his hands, he wove timelessness into physics and sliced atoms

with his fingernail. He inhaled comets into his mouth, and then expelled them into a vortex band of blackest obscurity. The traveler pulled molecules

together in order to make things materialize or smashed them, and they vaporized into speeding clusters of matter. Yet even he was not the Ultimate Reality

and the Supreme Original Existence. However, this stranger was given knowledge of the mystery of travelling souls and knew secrets of electro-magnetic energies of forests. Most trees of the forest, being more ancient, noticed his approach, and they trembled and convulsed. But the tallest most beautiful tree, being just an

infant and still living so much on impulse, could not decipher the coming of this stranger. Yet it didn't matter anyway, because his footsteps were slow and only

moved within the flow of the science of numbers. At that moment in infinity, his vision, X times stronger than infrared beams, fixated itself on the forest and the light

that wasn't a light. In his strong arms he held an ax sharpened by metallic gasses, its blade sharper than the sun's heat and its handle long and strong.

Who was this cosmic traveler, some asked as the forest swooned and its leaves rattled. The stranger stepped closer; and the Kingdom of the Alienated Forest, which

could never penetrate his cloaks of ambiguities, only knew him by the dreaded name ... the hewer of trees.

Entranced Dance

time dissipates
sounds cease
hunger, thirst
is a passing thing
the world melts

into the distance
I am lost inside
a strange trance
intoxicated on words
rushing in swirls
around my mind
causing this pen
to move in a wild dance

Senryu (Others)

others come and they
watch, materialize at
will, then disappear.

Poetic Rhapsody

Meter, trimeter, accents, and measures,
What melodious harmonies lyrics do capture!

Captivating tones produce a choir of words.
Feel the ballads striking balanced chords.

Heartstrings vibrate with musical poetry,
In unison with ebony and ivory harmony.

Words flow smoothly in iambic crescendo,
Pentameter, tetrameter, the magical tempo!

Sonant, poetic rhythmic verse,
Poignant, joyful, melancholy, or terse.

Brass and strings write a carefree rhapsody,
A quiet serenade or a spirited symphony.

Blow horns, beat drums in metric motion.
A chorus of words frees the imagination.

Hear, feel the earth's sublime melody.
Cadences of words gently set the heart free!

Song of the Wild Stallion

A furious runner!
Fierce and strong
Back of steel
Legs like iron
Burst of dust
As hooves strike ground
Blast of energy
Flies unbound
Sparks of fire
Emerge from his nose
Bravery and courage
Wherever he goes
His demeanor hints
He knows his strength
Royal and beautiful
His spirit rides free
A furious runner!
He was born to be

In the Blue Light

Floating in the womb of
faraway space,
drifting in the dawn's
dreaming arms, until
the resonance of shrill
pitches jolts my senses,

awakening me to cool
blue light. The unwelcome
visitor intrudes on my repose,
signaling the end of this
peaceful night.

Yelling in my window,
the nuisance bellows
like a tyrannical boss. My
body gives a toss here, there.

My mind resists the annoying
sounds. Frustration's
sighs make me rise from bed.
Hazy-headed,
body shivering, my bare feet
shuffle across chilly wood floors.

Desperation in search
of a clue to silence the
invader, whose piercing sounds
grow louder. I parted with

the last of the week-old
bread, which was greedily
snatched away.

Just like the other
mornings, that pesky
runt of a bird
again got its way.

Song of the Bee

Entice
me with
flowery fragrances,
delight my eyes with
beautiful colors, lavish
me with sweet nectar; and
I will always honor you with
the gift of satin flowing honey,
a flavor to make your buds blossom.
my healing wax is a soothing balm
from my honeycomb. Just don't
annoy my buzzing flights.
I have a stinging
temper.

Light

Yesterday, locked up rooms gave
the comfort of tidy dark, all
it ever knew.
Today, its grime and cobwebs outgrow
the shifting space, when glimmers
of light come
beaming through.
Tomorrow becomes the valley,
to choose between
the two.

The Room

"We are like rooms
waiting to be decorated:
some rooms overrun with
cobwebs of gloom,
others seedlings
waiting to bloom,
but the best one of all
is the room for improvement,"

said the crumpled poem from
the trash can.

Diamonds and Gold

Celebrate brightness of the sun
inside the beauty of your mind.
Celebrate hope's unique song,
music only your heart can find.

Celebrate the thirsty journey,
cooled by gifts of misty rain.
Celebrate the wings of faith
that strongly soar above the pain.

Celebrate green healing herbs
that sprout through solid ground.
Celebrate rainbow auras of light,
and wear them like a regal crown.

Celebrate those higher visions
that dance in joy and dignity.
Celebrate your childlike spirit,
alive in effervescent purity.

Celebrate dreams in your hand;
mold the gold to shine true.
Celebrate splendid sparks above;
those same diamonds live in you.

Tale of the Challenge of a Blank Page

White empty paper, pen in hand
Making words war with each other.
Mr. Pen scratches out that word,
Then makes this word bump out another.

Mr. Pen wants to eloquently write
Descriptive words on each line
To form deep vivid expressions,
But Mr. Word says, "Just make us rhyme!"

"Oh, come on, now," says Mr. Word,
"Insert that other word right here.
Mr. Pen, I don't believe you cannot see
That a rhyming line is so near."

"But, Mr. Word!" says Mr. Pen,
In a tone of impatient exasperation,
"Your words should clearly communicate
To stimulate thoughts of introspection."

"Phooey to all that cerebral stuff,"
Mr. Word angrily replies.
"I insist you make our sentences rhyme.
This is how we words show off our pride!"

"Okay," Mr. Pen reluctantly sighs.
"Mr. Word, have it your way,
Because I've reached the point now
Of listening to what you words have to say."

"Well, it's about time," says Mr. Word
As he haughtily sticks out his chest.
"Mr. Pen, sit back, take notes, and relax.
We words shall do all the rest.

"We will constantly attempt to crush
Your clichés and rambling, bumbling style.
It's a major struggling task for us,
And we words think it's terribly vile.

"Though, the fact is we need you, Mr. Pen,
To keep us in harmony when you write us out,
So when we have these little disagreements,
Please do not make your writings pout.

"We really do not want to be overly critical
Or to slice your ideas down to size.
We words are only sincerely trying
To make you keep that brain exercised!

"We words are not to be intimidating,
But yes, we possess shades of personality too.
When you do not know what to write,
Don't we assist you and show you what to do?"

"Okay, Mr. Word, I got it," responds Mr. Pen.
"You wisely settled a lot of things.
According to your advice, I will sit back, relax,
And let you words flutter your wings."

"So finally, we can get back to writing,"
With happy relief sighs Mr. Pen.
Mr. Word responds, "Yes, I also agree;
We shall bring this conversation to an end!"

Then, without warning, Mr. Pen just won't budge.
Mr. Word is very perplexed as to why.
After waiting a while, Mr. Word speaks up
And says with an exasperated sigh,

"Mr. Pen, come on and write. Why the delay?
Are you in agreement with our long talk?"
"Yes, of course I am," snaps Mr. Pen,
"But Ms. Hand just went for a walk!"

A Poem Never Knows

writing the poem is easiest,
a fun creative art.
to get folks to read and like it—
hmm ... that's the hardest part!

EPILOGUE

Leaves Upon the Wind

Oh trees,
I give thanks
to the Creator
for healing leaves.
Let them
speak in flight,
touched by
many pens,
so generations might
dance in valleys
and walk upon wind.

Notes

About the Author

Deborah Renee has worked with developmentally and physically disabled adults in direct care, and as a case manager and service coordinator. She has also taught reading and writing to adults in a literacy program. For the past several years, she has worked in direct care as a nursing assistant with AIDS patients and the elderly with Alzheimer's disease. She has loved poetry for many years, "always seeking to grow and expand in writing," and wrote poems as a hobby, having a few poems published in *Cat Fancy* magazine, *Writer's World, Network Africa* magazine, *Feelings*, and *Poet Sanctuary Reflections 2010*. She is currently studying in the field of Health Information Technology. She grew up in Sanford, Florida; Willingboro, New Jersey; and Philadelphia, Pennsylvania, where she currently resides. This is her first collection of published poems.

To contact author:

4privatewords@gmail.com